Good Son

Sundress Publications • Knoxville, TN

Editor: Sherrel McLafferty
Managing Editor: Tennison Black
Editorial Assistants: Kanika Lawton and Erin Elizabeth Smith
Editorial Interns: K Slade and Kenli Doss

Colophon: This book is set in Cormorant Garamond
Cover Art: "Koi Nobori" by Chemin Hsiao
Cover Design: Kristen Ton
Book Design: Sherrel McLafferty

Lorde epigraph is from *The Cancer Journals* by Audre Lorde, Penguin
Press New York, © 1980 by Audre Lorde.

Good Son

Kyle Liang

ACKNOWLEDGEMENTS

Thank you to the readers and editors of the following journals, who first published these poems.

Anomaly: "An ABC at a Birthday Party" and "An ABC in Question"
Best of the Net (2020): "A Lesson on Immunology"
Brooklyn Poets: "A Tracing of Our Shoeless Feet"
Crab Fat Magazine: "An ABC in a Dim Sum Restaurant"
Crab Fat Magazine: Best of Year Four: "An ABC in a Dim Sum Restaurant"
Diode: "Sudden Collapse" and "Synonyms"
Glass: A Journal of Poetry: "A Lesson on Immunology"
Hobart: "Self-Portrait as a Mouth" and "Reflux"
How to Build a House (Swan Scythe Press): "Reflux," "An ABC in a Dim Sum Restaurant," "I Can Eat Spicy," and "A Tracing of Our Shoeless Feet"
The Margins (Asian American Writers' Workshop): "She Sees a Video of a Mixed Girl Speaking Mandarin and, Confused, Says 'But That Girl Isn't Chinese'"
Stirring: "I Can Eat Spicy"
Tinderbox Poetry Journal: "No | Bùyào"
wildness: "A Translation of My Body" and "ROMI"

CONTENTS

I

II

III

for Morgan

"What are the tyrannies you swallow day by day and attempt to make your own, until you will sicken and die of them, still in silence?"
—Audre Lorde

I

GOOD SON

You'll wind up housing a skeleton of fish
in your stomach if you don't slow down

she preaches from beside her teeth-cleaned bones.
And I'll be the one who must remove them.

I watch her spit what can't be eaten,
which isn't much. I try to recreate the motion

of her cheeks and lips, deconstruct the instinct
of finding food as if I've gone hungry before

too. A pair of my checkered underwear hanging
outside fights the wind. As if I need reminding,

she tells me to drink the soup she made.
Like a good son, I don't hesitate to sip

loudly, searching the bottom of the bowl for more
gǒu qǐ zi. She isn't looking, so I sip louder.

The pile of bones in front of me hopelessly small—
flesh still clinging to the carcass, unwilling to be gnawed off

by my American mouth. I wonder how much
I've even swallowed. My mother opens her throat

again, whiplashes of wind surround the house,
summoning all things in its direction.

SELF-PORTRAIT AS A MOUTH

My mother speaks to me in scissors.
She runs each blade down the lobe of my ear.

Father sits in the corner staring
as if expecting me to cry but hoping

he raised a man and not a boy.
The stains on my shirt from dinner

dye the fabric a new color. Instead
of white I am dressed in what's left.

The other kids laugh directly in my face,
their grins wrap around my neck

like a car around a telephone pole.
I want to go. I want to go. I want to

go, but the only place I can is inside. So I
hook my fingers into the sides of my mouth

and swallow myself.

REFLUX

We walked to the edge of the continent / and there in the sand I turned to her and said / look, this is where I buried myself // It's the only place on earth / where the water doesn't reflect // I begged it to end until it finally gave in // Behind us are the trees that watched me / stab my shovel into the ground // Their limbs turn with the wind / and I don't blame them // Before she can stop me I drop to my knees / begin grabbing handfuls of sand / and shoving them into my mouth // What are you doing, she yells // I swallow // What are you doing // I swallow // What are you doing // I swallow // She tears at my arms like a mother / who caught her child with one of the bottles / from her personal cabinet // Stop that, she cries // I cough a cloud / The sand abrades my throat // In severe cases of reflux the esophagus will undergo metaplasia / in order to develop tissue / similar to that of the cardia / If my stomach bleeds enough it will become an ocean // The wind stops and the tree limbs shift back into place / I don't blame them

SHE SEES A VIDEO OF A MIXED GIRL SPEAKING MANDARIN AND, CONFUSED, SAYS "BUT THAT GIRL ISN'T CHINESE"

Every night I dream of being
washed away in the waves
of a Taiwan Strait—rinsed
from the mouths of my family,

salt-filled cheeks, my eyes
tearing off into the moonlight.
Father only tells stories
when I ask him. *Where were you*

stationed in the mountains?
Did you dream of America
or survival? Which kept you alive?
Which almost killed you?

Yesterday,
I tucked Yé yé into bed.
As I laid him down,
straightened his legs,

he whispered
the last words
he could remember
in English. *Take it*

easy. So, I drew the sheet
over his body
stopping at his neck.
For now

I still make jokes
about the Chinese
            restaurants like our last
one on Town Street. I'll tell

            my white friends
there are only two requirements,
            an adjective & a noun:
Golden Chopsticks,

            Elegant Dragon,
Lucky Star.
            Maybe if they understand
our names then they'll stop

            calling me Ching Chong
when I drag the duck sauce
            smell to school. The last time
I was in New York

            someone's son asked
how tall I am. He was really asking
            where I fit. If I have a son
with his mother's eyes

            will there be room for me
under his tongue?
            Will he want to eat
bitter squash just because

            it's what Daddy did?
I make myself small
            on subways & elevators,
lay my life out

in the corner, nestle under
the paw of a tiger. The women
        in my family only know how
to raise Mongolian-spotted children—

        blackish blue, bruised
in appearance. As a child,
        my mother clawed
sheets of skin off my back

        so I could be striped
like the other kids.
        So my vertebrae
could grieve openly.

        My Mongolian spot
refuses to fade. I guess
        some of us will always
look like abused children.

        In school I learned trauma
will stall a person's development.
        In school I learned some of us
will always look like abused children.

AN ABC AT A BIRTHDAY PARTY

yesterday i spent an hour looking at the census
to see if we really are as small as my teachers
make me feel. even at the birthday party
they insisted on throwing to celebrate
my arrival on this planet, nobody wanted
to be there. there were limp balloons
in all my least favorite colors, envelopes
full of gift cards to stores i never shop at,

        no one asked what music i wanted
so the dj played toby keith requests while i sat
in the corner waiting for cotton-eyed joe
to leave the back of my teeth.

     at the end of the night
i stood by the door thanking guests
as they left. halfway through i noticed
my lips were saying i'm sorry instead.

my teachers lined up along
the perimeter to watch me fold
empty chairs and stack them
where they said. *we saved you*
a piece of cake they hissed.
sarah is bringing the rest back
to her kids. they haven't eaten
dessert yet. make sure you shut off
all the lights before you pop the balloons.
we'll leave you a knife to use. and by the way,
happy birthday. the door shuts.

MY FATHER HOWLS AS HE TELLS ME ABOUT THE NIGHT
HE TOOK A BATHROOM BREAK WHILE PATROLLING THE
MILITARY BASE AND HEARD A SINGLE GUNSHOT ERUPT
FROM THE STALL NEXT TO HIM

causing the metal door to fall open
unable to support
the dead weight
of a five-foot-tall
one hundred and fifty pound
bag of rice

AN ABC IN A DIM SUM RESTAURANT

the door opens and a bell rings. grandma walks in followed by grandpa followed by grandmas left leg.[1] i jump to my feet and anxiously stand behind the chair.[2] i wait forty-seven seconds for grandma. her leg dragging on the carpet behind her.[3] i rush to the other side to pull out a chair. i pull out another for grandpa. i hug grandpa. i hug grandma long enough for her to say *bǎo bèi bǎo bèi wǒ de bǎo bèi* three times as a tide of tears washes over her with excitement to see her grandson.[4]

i rush back to my seat and grab their tea cups to wipe clean with my cloth napkin before they have a chance to reach for them.[5] i carefully pour out the steaming chrysanthemum tea perhaps burning myself in the process.[6] i smile at them. they smile back. grandpa gives me a thumbs up and both him and grandma tell me im handsome. i thank them. they smile. i smile.[7]

---

1. Grandma suffered a stroke in 1995 followed by another several years later
2. A salute to a life of suffering
3. How we describe weight as dead when it's heaviest
4. Followed by silence. The space between me and her seated, now only half-mobile, torso apparent
5. Eager to please
6. Guaranteeing another person's health and happiness at the cost of one's own is the greatest form of endearment
7. Being the only Chinese boy in my class, I told my parents that Mandarin is useless so I refused to speak it. A few years later, I forgot how to speak it altogether, severing my ability to communicate with my grandparents

mom slaps my leg under the table as i look around the restaurant.[8] i look at grandma and grandpa. they feel my eyes and turn their heads to meet my face with another smile. this time drool starts to leak from the corner of grandmas mouth.[9] she reaches for the glob with the tissue in her right hand and wipes it away as if its the thousandth time today. it might be. a baby can be heard crying on the other side of the restaurant.

the bell rings. dad walks in smelling of home depot. he is covered in paint and saw dust.[10] he sits down and begins eating. i take his cup in my hand before he has a chance to think about how thirsty he is and begin wiping and pouring more of the hot chrysanthemum tea.[11]

the waitress comes over and drops off the slippery rice noodle roll that mom ordered when no one was paying attention.[12] i quickly take the two wooden disposable chopsticks out of their paper sleeve and rub them together like im trying to start a fire.[13]

---

8. Mom hates when I shake my leg under the table
9. One side of grandma's face does not smile
10. His fingers are probably bleeding and the cracks of his palms are permanently packed with dirt. He drops his parents off in front of the restaurant before finding parking so that they do not have to walk across the parking lot
11. Making sure not to let out the most bitter tasting tea at the bottom of the pot
12. Grandma's favorite
13. Disposable wooden chopsticks are rubbed together to remove any potential splinters

i use the ends to cut the roll into sections which i then distribute around the table. first to grandma then to grandpa then to dad then to mom and then to me. i ask if anyone is thirsty. grandpa replies that he wants beer. grandma says she wants water.[14] i rehearse what im going to say to the waitress in my head before standing up and yelling our familys order to her in mandarin only to find out that she speaks cantonese.[15]

---

14. Warm water

15. A failure to overcompensate

SELF-PORTRAIT AS A FISH

I speak to my mother every week—
                her to me in Chinese, me to her
     in English, not knowing if I can still string
sentences in Mandarin as beautifully as I did
        when I was three & only knew how to ask
for answers.

     It's funny what our throats remember
now that I'm old enough to answer.
              I'm forced to fall back
on the sounds I can make, the notes
I haven't forgotten how to play.

                Hǎo. Good. *Hěn hǎo.* Very good.
     Máfan. Troublesome, a burden.

             I answer my mother's friends
like a fractured song. *I'm good. I'm very good.*
    I'm very, very good. I'm hoping
            no one asks a question I can't answer.

To avoid embarrassment, I've practiced
                redirecting inquiries to be about my family.
        When asked where I'm from,
             I say my mom is from Malaysia,
dad is from Taiwan. When asked what I speak,
                I say *we* speak Mandarin

at home. I rehearse the same Chinese phrases
             again and again,
      repeating after my interviewer when I can.
           Are you finished with school? *I'm finished*

with school. Do you live here in New York?
                    I live here in New York.
My mouth, like water, taking the shape
                                of their vocal cords.

I laugh at jokes exposing our frugality,
        write poetry retelling our family's displacement,
close my fingers into a fist
                when I hear locals teasing tourists
with only enough English to ask
        for a picture.

I speak of being Chinese
        even though my tongue cannot distinguish
                rain, *yǔ*, from fish, *yú*,
        & my hands sometimes forget
                to guard the teapot to avoid letting anyone
fill their own cup without me first noticing.

        I speak of being Chinese because here,
they'll call a dog a fish
                if it doesn't bark.

AN ABC IN QUESTION

You ask me what I eat at home
so I tell you I feed on ghosts

of my ancestors who saved me
all the best pieces. You ask me

what I speak when with my family
so I tell you battle codes.

I tell you paper boats.
I tell you it's something

you wouldn't want
to understand. Yet

you keep asking me.
You want to know why

I look like I'm always squinting
and laugh when I respond

it's because I don't know
who I can trust. You insist

on tracing your tongue along
my skin in search of something,

anything, you won't like.
An anxious reminder

your instinct was right.
It doesn't taste good

but at least you can say
I tried. You can

close your trusty eyes tonight
certain of their judgement.

And I'll fall asleep
with one eye open.

A LESSON ON IMMUNOLOGY

let go of my throat
so I can cough

free your fear
from my trachea

my diaphragm
is exploding

I step onto the subway
with white flags

tacked to my skin
I whisper to my nose

begging *please*

don't run
then take ten paces

to the nearest empty seat
my mom calls

to tell me the Chinese aunties
are sharing videos on WeChat

of Asians in white masks
getting their lungs

ripped out their chests
by white men searching

for weapons of mass
destruction she cries

there's no use

in wearing white
masks in public

we're under attack
either way

our bodies at war
with the world

and a virus

so I close my eyes
and imagine a day

I no longer feel like a guest
in my own country

I hold my breath waiting

for when I'm the host
and not the pathogen

I CAN EAT SPICY

This morning, I put on a silk shirt.
Last night, I shampooed my hair with persimmons

until the drain asked if I was bleeding
yellow from trying to clean my greasy perm.

If you close your eyes, black tea tastes just
as good as Coca-Cola, so I call the waitress over

by standing in the middle of a dim sum restaurant,
shouting my order loud enough

to break the silence that follows me
into every conversation with my grandparents.

Tonight, I'll rest my head on scallion pancakes
and try to dream of dragons dancing over a fence.

Goodnight, sixth-grade self.
Tomorrow, we'll play more games

and maybe next time,
you won't want to be the cowboy.

II

A TRACING OF OUR SHOELESS FEET

I somehow always see my mom when she's waiting at the bus stop in the ocean

I watch the waves nearly toss her over before walking up and asking

Momma don't you know the bus doesn't come down here anymore

I forget she doesn't know English too well so I paraphrase

Momma not today

Yet I still stand next to her beside that metal sign and together we let the current push and pull our bodies dressed in soaking clothes

The weight of the water pulls our shoes off

While we wait she tells me stories of how grandpa used to sell bowls of handmade noodles for three dollars

Or was it three ringgits

It was three ringgits

Anyways she tells me how he used to walk across a tight rope of barbed wire with bare feet while he held a bowl in one hand and rang a bell in the other because one day a farmer came up to him and said a three ringgit bowl sounds less sad if you ring a bell while you sell it so take this bell I took from my best cow and may it help you feed your children

Ring ding ding   ding ding ding ding   ding   ding ding

Someone tell brother the bus isn't coming

I liked Sungai Buloh but it's hot and my feet were starting to look like grandpa's the way they never callused

I was afraid my toes would fall off like the end of a cigarette

At school the teachers made us go outside and walk tiny circles around dead pigeons that flew into the window hoping to be inside

I know something you don't know

The fastest way into the city is actually by boat

There is a river that runs upstream from the dirt floor kitchen to JP Morgan

Rock beats scissor and scissor beats paper but paper beats a boat full of starving children who use sleep to forget about their stomachs

When is a boat considered an island

When do you become a person

Do you know that question if you were stranded alone on an island and could only bring three things then what would they be

What would you bring to an island that is overpopulated

I think I'll ask that on my next date

My wife better know how to swim

I sometimes swim for hours

I sometimes fear I will have to choose between swimming and swallowing

I swallow and choke on the hypervigilance I was spoon fed by my parents

If I'm choking to death then don't try to save me just ask the doctor who does the autopsy not to dress me in glasses and suspenders and take pictures of my shrunken genitals trying to reaffirm any of his preconceived notions after I can't defend myself

Ask the doctor if he will instead cut open my chest and reach into my lungs for an alveolus

Ask the doctor to dissect the membranous sac and see that inside is a tiny me naked and crying

I was born a tree that was quickly cut down and had his name changed to wood

I was born from the times my mom found out that I was bullying back and made me peel the stickers off a globe then asked me to point to where we're from

The geography category at bar trivia has become my least favorite

I somehow point to the Milky Way as a place between Ethiopia and Ghana

I circle Orion's Belt when my finger traces up the east of China in search of Japan

With over one hundred billion stars in the universe who gets to name all of them

Who decides what clusters have significance

Or do the one hundred billion not exist unless someone writes their names down on paper

PROPERTY LINE

No one told me I couldn't lay here so here I am, laid across this border, waiting for the sea to take my body from the shore or for the police to take turns gnawing my flesh like flies, telling me which parts I can keep and which are illegal. No one gave me permission, but no one said there needed to be permission granted either. I can lay like this for years. I can live in the shelter of the birds overhead until you finally decide what to call this. Barely living. Half alive. The salt water pulling at my wet legs as if to drag me. The sand under my torso carved out like a coffin weakly anchoring me to land. A white man walking the beach with his daughter stop when they see my blistering body, limbs laying how I last left them. They decide to help, so they rush home and bring back a homemade sign that says *For Sale*. They drive it into the sand beside my head and proudly wait. The father looks down at his daughter and smiles. She thinks to herself, perhaps I should do a good deed for someone every day. Perhaps I should become a senator. What better way to perform random acts of kindness than with more lies. Her mother—his wife—arrives and feeds me water from the ocean, scooping it into my mouth with her empty glass wine bottle. She makes me hypertonic. She makes me demyelinate. Water retreats from my brain to correct the concentration. My parenchyma shrinks. I retreat from my body and leave them with what they were looking for when they found me in the first place.

DISTURBAN

We are sitting in a library. Cut. No, we are sitting in an oven. Better. Action. We are sitting in an oven, on public WiFi, paying rent online in wingdings. Why wingdings? Why not. The landlord decided two years ago that tenants would give up deciphering all their housing paperwork, so by the time they understood how to make a payment they would just do it without asking questions. Question: should everyone be wearing duck costumes in this scene? Yes. Let's make everyone wear duck costumes. Action. We are in an oven, everyone is dressed as ducks, the sound of their fat sizzling is mouthwatering. It's irresistible. The crackle is making us, the viewers, go mad. We're all mad. We're so mad that we are salivating from our pores. Our eyes are drooling. Big, thick puddles form around our feet. It looks like we're crying, but we're not. We're just insatiable. We're like dogs. Or are dogs like us? Cut. Action. We are a pack of rabid dogs watching roasted ducks cook in an oven just before the broil.

NONMALEFICENCE

I told the doctor my brother and I are hungry. So he told us to eat our feet. But sir, I said, if we eat our feet then how will we walk home. He told us to make a boat with our bodies and sail home. You can go back to where you came from, he said. You can leave your mother's uterus in your place. Consider it a trade. Two bodies for creation. My mother, not knowing what she was agreeing to, agreed. But momma, he's going to take your uterus. What's my uterus, she asked. I cried into her dress. I told the doctor my mother can't provide informed consent. What's informed consent, he asked. I cried again. A nurse took my brother and I by the hand and walked us down a hallway. We asked her where we were going. We asked where she was taking us. Shhhh, it's spread through droplets, the nurse said sweetly, and placed duct tape over our mouths. The hallway lights became less yellow and more white the further we walked. Soon we were standing in a laboratory with four men in hazmat suits. By the time we noticed there was no one holding our hands, the nurse was gone. We've got two kung flus, one said in a muffled voice, presumably into a walkie talkie or radio. We'll start with the smaller of the two. I thrashed as they grabbed me by the armpits and I looked back at my brother who they began spraying with a hose. I cried into the sterile sleeve of one of the hazmat suits as my shoes skidded across the floor. My stomach rumbled and I thought of my mother's dress.

A TRANSLATON OF MY BODY

At the beach, I normally don't go
past neck deep. If I can't search

the ground with my feet then
I'll start swallowing water

before it swallows me. Under
the ocean is a canopy of hands

grabbing at what it thinks is air,
inadvertently making fists.

Have you noticed how
we refer to water as a body

then write laws
on how to govern it?

I should rewrite my body.
I should give myself a nose

this time, replace my bones
with something that floats.

In a translation of my body,
floating is all that matters.

III

FISTS

Dogs will grow to fit their paws
Men grow to fit their fists
I choose my words like a surgeon
who knows his job is to cut

NOMENCLATURE

We give what we can afford.
We afford what we can. We can
tear a cow to shreds and call it steak
tips, place a napkin on our laps and say
it's fine dining; a dog is a dog
but his sister's a bitch. Humans
are patients when their bodies
become answerless. Death is given
a time—pronounced,
as if there is a right and wrong
way to speak of parting.
I call their families after
speaking in silences.
I call with a plan
of how many times to utter *I'm sorry*
before they think I did it.
My parents take turns trying
to describe how I look different
when I return for Thanksgiving:
atrophied, masked facies, symptomatic.
In medicine, we call the things
we don't understand idiopathic,
the problems we cause iatrogenic.
We are expected to have a name,
an answer, for everything.
Do you know what happens
to banana trees who grow the most?
Their hands are cut off
when everyone's hungry.

POEM IN WHICH NOTHING BAD HAPPENS AT ALL

This is not a poem in which bad things happen and definitely not
because of me. I learn which letters to capitalize in a poem title
instead of capitalizing every letter. In this poem
all my friends are really strong readers by eighth grade so
when our teacher calls on them I don't have to worry
that they're going to stutter or mispronounce certain words.
There is never a shooting at the bar down the street
from my middle school. In fact
there are no shootings. The pool party at my house doesn't result in
Chris' New Era fitted getting thrown into the water.
The brim stays dry and stiff and I intervened as soon as
I saw a hand reach for it when he wasn't paying attention.
Instead of throwing a right hook into my brother's cheek,
in this poem I tell my brother what a good job he's doing
at raising me while our parents are working. At work,
instead of telling the nurse that it's fine if we don't
draw another lactate, I tell her to draw another lactate,
it's really important we draw another lactate
and send it to the lab on ice this time
because I suspect it's going to be elevated,
which it is, so I bolus a liter of IV fluids and order a CT scan
which reveals meters of necrotic black bowel
and I immediately consult colorectal surgery
who bring her to the OR emergently and
remove all of the diseased loops of intestine
and she lives this time. She is still alive today. Probably
somewhere with her family.
In this poem I sleep great.
Dogs don't bite.
Only gently nibble.
My grandmother never has a stroke.

My grandfather remembers everyone
right up until he dies. I never walk
in on him hitting my grandmother
with her cane while she sits defenselessly
half paralyzed from the first stroke.
In this poem I am grateful for all the bad things
that never happened.

MEAT
for vegans

Meat is another word for memory.
Or memorabilia. I used to grill
my memories, fry them, bake
then broil them, toss them
in a wok with ginger and garlic.
Pay extra for better memories.
I used to take my time chewing
every shadow of its flesh until
the juices refused
and consumption
was the only answer left.
Taste and tenderness.
Red in the center
like a memory.
Bleeding just enough
like a memory. Once,
I licked my fingers clean
of the memories. Only once.
I thought I needed memories.
Couldn't go a day without,
until I learned they haunt
your body even after
you swallow them all.

NIGHT SHIFT

It doesn't take much to wake me up at 3 am.
A subtle drop in temperature or pressure,
the sound of the top sheet against the duvet cover,
a dream I didn't ask for. There is no escape
living in a 550-square-foot apartment
so I commute from the bed to the couch
and if I'm feeling particularly lonely,
the dinner table. I know the light won't come
for a few more hours and once it does, I can't hide,
thus, I'll leave the lights off until I'm cornered.
I'll make my own sun with my laptop,
illuminate my face, neck, and bare chest
as it rests on my thighs the way it was intended,
drafting emails I won't send for hours,
reading anything I can find online in the dark.
I consider going back to bed but give up
on the idea of sleep and focus on the warmth
from my overheating computer sitting on my skin.
Perhaps I'll lay on the couch and let it press
against my stomach or sternum or even
collarbone. On these nights, I listen
to the sound of my breath and imagine
how nice it must be to rest your head
on another's thighs or chest, to be asked
to come back to bed.

SUDDEN COLLAPSE
    After Body Elite Gym at the corner of Court Street and
    Union Street

Yesterday a three-story building in Carroll Gardens collapsed

Locals say the walls had been bowing
for months   *bulging* over the sidewalk

Passersby walked around it like a slow-growing puddle

Nothing
worth stopping for

Everyone in Brooklyn already asking
what will replace it

Perhaps a new Trader Joe's
or coffee shop

An entrance is created by an exit
wound

I imagine the bricks exploded upon impact

—a violent red-brown
plume of dust   The aftermath

of an infrastructure that retaliated
against itself   In Taipei

my father and I rode in the backseat of a taxi
past all his favorite childhood spots in awe

He pointed out how buildings aged
from top to bottom—

businesses built on top of one another to save space

Generations standing on each other's shoulders

A brighter view of the skyline closer to the sun

THE HILLS

My childhood house sits in a neighborhood
of hills that resemble knuckles.

I drive home for the holidays
over a bed of roads—

cracked
and softened from years of use.

Some turns still sound like police sirens.
When my tires skid on certain corners, I shudder

like an engine in winter
trying not to fail.

The mailboxes silently judge
the way I drive past children

crossing signs. I try not to
remember that snowy October

all the trees fell on our houses,
reaching into our upstairs

bedrooms, opening us
to the dark cold.

TRUST ISSUES

When my hometown friends
tell me it'll be fine,
I don't question it.
I just get in
the car and trust

their flawed judgement.
The way the road twists
and disappears into
the trees. Smoke
from the party vanishing

between the seams
of my jeans. Skin still
vibrating from the girl
who thought I was cute
enough to flirt with

while her ex pretended
not to watch me
every time I was alone
and convinced myself
vodka Gatorade cocktails

could make up for his size
advantage.
But if he told me
he'd kick my ass,
I'd trust him. Unlike

the guys at my college.
I stopped trusting them the night
one dropped their shoulder
into my boy's chest
but refused to throw hands

when my boy asked
him to step outside.
They say you can't trust
anyone with no flaws,
which is why I trust my friends

from home and no one else.
We left the bar
early that night.
Fuck those fucking kids,
man, he said shakily,

steering his voice back
into his chest.
It's because I'm fucking brown.
They think they're fucking
better than me.

SYNONYMS

Where I'm from, summer storms bring carpets
of bunker fish carcasses to shore.

When heavy rain falls, the fish all swim
the same direction toward shallow waters,

suffocating themselves and each other. Sadly,
it is instinct to crave the taste of salt. And

in the body, water follows salt.
In the body, excess salt causes retention.

Lungs fill like two waterlogged barrels
when we retain. They say it feels like drowning.

They say the right answer is often the simplest.
What is the difference between drowning and

suffocating? If I drown my fists into the earth then
what will grow next spring? The difference

between drowning and flooding is the subject. Perhaps
the better question is when the flood is coming,

and who will be next to me when it rains.

NO	BÙYÀO
this house is not	zhè gè jiā bù shì
a boat & we	yī sōu chuán
are not here	wǒ mén bù kě yǐ
to steer you	sòng nǐ
back to kaohsiung	huí qù
grandpa	yé yé
unpack your bags	fàng xià nǐ de dōng xī
the doctor is waiting	yī shēng děng zhe nǐ
he wants to see you	tā yào nǐ
draw a clock	huà huà
he wants to hear you	rán hòu tā yào tīng nǐ
talk to father	jiǎng huà
so they can translate	
your words	
to years that fit	
inside their mouths too	
i know	wǒ zhī dào
we are asking	má fán
a lot	
after all	
how does one cure	
a sickness that lives	

in today
when he cannot

how does one beg
their hands

to turn off
a stove

if their fingers
only remember

how to bait
a hook

kě shì nǐ xū yào

ROMI

It's June 18th, 2020 and my father tells me his chest feels *uncomfortable*. I ask if he's dyspneic. He says it isn't that. I probably shouldn't use my hospital words so I ask him how long he can close his eyes before realizing how hollow his lungs are. There's a pause. He sighs. The phone is pressed so tight against my ear his next breath empties me like a straw. My father tells me he feels *uncomfortable* every time he walks past grandpa's belongings still around the house. He says he can't breathe. He says *bú shūfú*. Very *bú shūfú*. As he continues talking, I realize it might be happening right now so I start loading questions—does it happen any other time? how long does it last for? are you in pain?—but wait to open fire because we're taught to let patients reveal their diagnosis by not interrupting. We call it good history taking. When my grandfather died on June 16th, 2020 I found out his birth name was Cheng Yu Liang. However when he came to the U.S. they left out the g from its spelling, making him Cheng Yu Lian. Our family's history taken upon arrival.

V

RAIN

There was still an hour before dusk.
You laid sideways on the bed—
knees curled toward your chest,
head anchored to my ribs—
our bodies meeting like a cross.

We were a soundless thought.
I measured our years together
in promises
& counted the places
on my body where you've been.

I love moments like this, you said.
The rain outside picked up.
Me too.

I held your gaze like a sweet
red bean under my tongue.
Your forehead warmed my lips
as I kissed it & my fingers traced
the space between each of yours.

Above, a tumble of clouds found us.
Its thunder dulling our distractions.

I was encased by it. Encased by the rain.
Sunken by the storm. The weight of
your head stationing me under
you.

And we posed like pictures
under laminate scrapbook pages
as every leaf on every branch
on every tree in the yard outside
bobbed under the downpour.

SUMMER

Some summer nights I want to strip down
and skate across the clouds
I want to beat the first light and surrender
to the thinning atmosphere
I want the air to be so cold that the blood shunts
from my legs and arms to my heart
so it beats with a fullness I have yet to know
I want my heart to be greedy again

PATIENCE

Patience is learned after it's broken
You could say the same thing about love
I love the way our toes touch under the covers
even when we go to bed mad
Our bodies eventually curling together
like leaves in winter
I love when we say goodbye
Not because we're saying goodbye
but because our foreheads collapse
like two logs over an open fire
warm embers

BIRDS

Ask me whose fists I father   My love
ask how the violence of the birds

I shot and killed as a boy still haunts me
and how long it's been since I last ate one

Dogs pass me waiting
for which of us will bark first

Our jowls stirring with impatience
I pray for parts that make me human

enough   I accept the thunder and rain
How the sun on wet cement after

a storm recovers smells and leaves us
with a taste we can almost name

I am grateful for all that happened
because all that happened brought me you

TWILIGHT

After returning from work
in the morning, I remove my scrubs,
leaving them in a bag by the door.
I rinse off in the shower
then slowly ease into bed
on my side.

You crawl up from behind
and lovingly cling to my body
like a heavy wool coat
whose weight rests perfectly
against the backs of my shoulders.
Your soft, warm breath diffusing
the back of my neck.

This is how I fall asleep each day
with you, my twilight.
You, my midnight sun,
scattering into me.
Our bodies refracting,
lighter
beside each other.

NOTES

In Chinese, the number four (sì) sounds similar to death (sǐ), making four an unlucky number in Chinese culture. Hence why there is no fourth section of this book.

"ABC," pronounced "A, B, C," stands for "American-Born Chinese"—a widely-used term to describe individuals of Chinese descent who are born and raised in America.

"Reflux" refers to the medical phenomenon known as Barrett's esophagus, in which chronic, repetitive, and injurious exposure of stomach acid to the esophageal lining from long-term gastroesophageal reflux disease (GERD) causes damage and, in some cases, transformation of esophageal cells into cells morphologically similar to the stomach, thereby increasing the risk of esophageal cancer.

"My Father Howls as He Tells Me About the Night He Took a Bathroom Break While Patrolling the Military Base and Heard a Single Gunshot Erupt from the Stall Next to Him" highlights the Republic of China's compulsory military service known as conscription. From its initiation in 1949 until the 21st century, all Taiwanese men were required to serve a minimum of two to three years. This was, however, shortened to one year and then, eventually, four months. In 2023, the laws changed once again, this time extending the mandatory length of service. As of January 1, 2024, all Taiwanese men born after January 1, 2005 are required to serve for one year. Data on the average height and weight of adult Taiwanese men was obtained from the study "Anthropometric Characteristics in Taiwanese Adults: Age and Gender Differences" by Chen et al (2021).

"A Lesson on Immunology" was written in March 2020 in response to the rising number of Asian hate crimes in the United States.

"Property Line" references osmotic demyelination syndrome—a life-threatening neurologic complication caused by the rapid overcorrection of hyponatremia, during which brain cells attempt to regulate a sudden change in sodium concentration.

"Nonmaleficence" includes the terms nonmaleficence and informed consent, which is the obligation of medical providers to do no harm to patients and the agreement between patients and medical providers to undergo medical interventions on the basis that the patient has reasonable understanding of the treatment and the decision-making capacity, respectively. The poem also includes the phrase "kung flu," first used by former President of the United States Donald Trump at a rally in Tulsa, Oklahoma in June 2020 when describing the COVID-19 pandemic that was understood to originate from Wuhan, People's Republic of China.

"Sudden Collapse" uses language from the article "3-Story Building in Brooklyn That Housed Gym Suddenly Collapses" by Matthew Haag.

"Poem in Which Nothing Bad Happens at All" was written after Jameson Fitzpatrick's "Poem in Which Nothing Bad Ever Happens To Me."

"ROMI" is an acronym for "rule out myocardial infarction," which describes patients with reasonably high suspicion for an acute coronary syndrome or "heart attack" based on their clinical presentation and risk factors and therefore monitored in a hospital setting.

THANK YOUS

A very big thank you to my publisher, Sundress Publications. You published one of my first poems, "I Can Eat Spicy," and it feels right that you now published my first full-length collection. Thank you, Tenni, Erin, and everyone at Sundress for all your hard work. Thank you, Sherrel, for your tremendous care, attention, and patience while editing this book with me. I learned so much through this process. You made me a better poet.

When I think of poetry, I think of Jason Koo. This book would not be possible without his support and the Brooklyn Poets community. Koo—thank you for your example, guidance, and friendship over the past decade. I'm not sure who or where I'd be as a poet had we not met during my time as an undergraduate health science major at Quinnipiac. And to the Brooklyn Poets community—you are the best. Thank you for finding each other and for finding me. Cheers to our city.

To Jennifer Huang and Laura Kolbe—thank you both for graciously agreeing to read *Good Son* and taking the time to write blurbs. To have your words on the back of my book is an absolute gift, one that I cherish deeply.

To all my past and present students—thank you for teaching me more than I could ever teach you. I'm so proud of all of you.

To my dear friend Keith—I am forever indebted to you for your wisdom on life, love, family, country, identity, education, work, writing, war, peace, politics, philosophy, religion, and all things under (and beyond) the sun, which has opened the world to me and me to the world. You believed in me before I believed in myself, and now I'm in a position to do the same for others. I owe much of this to you. Thank you.

To my high school English teacher Dr. Bierman—thank you for teaching me what it means to write, to surrender yourself to this practice and craft, many years ago.

To the Moschettas—thank you for welcoming me into your family and caring for me in more ways than I could ever ask for, whether it's making sure there are always vegan dishes at the table or recreating American childhood experiences I didn't know I missed out on.

To my incredible coworkers at New York-Presbyterian/Weill-Cornell—thank you for braving 2020 and on with me. Thank you for being my support system during those sad, scary, trying times. Thank you for being my friends in the big city. Thank you for being my work family. Thank you for sharing so much of your lives with me and being such a big part of mine.

To all my friends—thank you for being here. The world needs you more than you know. I need you more than you know.

To Taiwan—the world sees you and stands with you.

To Tián Tián and Mì Mì—Shū Shu loves you.

To Mom, Dad, Kevin, and Steph—thank you for empowering me with your overwhelming, oftentimes undeserving, love. It is an inexhaustible source of inspiration.

Lastly, to my wife Morgan—if love is the answer to the problem of human existence, then I am grateful you are my answer. I spent the first twenty years of my life trying to understand where I belong, and now I know, it is with you. I love you now more than ever.

ABOUT THE AUTHOR

Kyle Liang is the son of Taiwanese and Malaysian immigrants. He is the author of the chapbook *HOW TO BUILD A HOUSE* (Swan Scythe Press, 2018), and his work has appeared in *Best of the Net*, Asian American Writers' Workshop's *The Margins, Glass: A Journal of Poetry, wildness, Diode*, and elsewhere. In addition to working as a physician assistant at New York-Presbyterian/Weill Cornell, Kyle teaches at Quinnipiac University and Brooklyn Poets. He is an avid vegan, climber, and Knicks fan. Kyle lives with his wife Morgan in New York City.

OTHER SUNDRESS TITLES

Ruin & Want
José Angel Araguz
$17.99

Nocturne in Joy
Tatiana Johnson-Boria
$12.99

Age of Forgiveness
Caleb Curtiss
$12.99

Another Word for Hunger
Heather Bartlett
$12.99

Little Houses
Athena Nassar
$12.99

Where My Umbilical is Buried
Amanda Galvan Huynh
$12.99

In Stories We Thunder
V. Ruiz
$12.99

the Colored page
Matthew E. Henry
$12.99

Slack Tongue City
Mackenzie Berry
$12.99

Year of the Unicorn Kidz
jason b. crawford
$12.99

Sweetbitter
Stacey Balkun
$12.99

Something Dark to Shine In
Inès Pujos
$12.99

www.ingramcontent.com/pod-product-compliance
Lightning Source LLC
Chambersburg PA
CBHW031150090426
42738CB00008B/1288